written by Nthabi Faku-Juqula

illustrated by Palesa Juqula

(Told through the eyes of Nthabi's six-year-old granddaughter, Nehanda)

Conscious Dreams
PUBLISHING

Lockdown at Gogo's

Copyright ©2023: Nthabi Faku-Juqula & Nehanda Juqula-Campbell

All rights reserved. No part of this publication may be produced, distributed, or transmitted in any form or by any means, including photocopying, recording, or other electronic or mechanical methods, without the prior written permission of the publisher, except in the case of brief quotations embodied in critical reviews and certain other non-commercial uses permitted by copyright law.

First Printed in United Kingdom 2023

Published by Conscious Dreams Publishing

Illustrated by Palesa Juqula

Edited by Daniella Blechner

Typeset by Bryony Dick

www.consciousdreamspublishing.com

@consciousdreamspublishing

ISBN: 978-1-915522-28-3

My sister and I always visit my Gogo in Tottenham during holidays; that is, if we haven't gone on holiday outside of the country, which has not happened since the pandemic. Also, some school holidays are spent with Gogo. In March of this year, however, we visited because, like all big events with Gogo, we spent Mother's Day with her. Or should I refer to it as 'Grandma's Day'. She was excited because it was a chance for her to enjoy breakfast in bed made by someone else, and she got Mother's Day cards and flowers, which she loved a lot. I'm sometimes envious of all the presents she gets. On that day, she spent the day chilling, with my mum fussing over her, and us enjoying the activities that accompanied the day.

This time round, whilst enjoying a few days with Gogo, there was an announcement from the government which said there was going to be a lockdown because of a new virus called coronavirus. So, we were stuck in Tottenham. I was told it was okay to stay put at Gogo's house because we were 'in a bubble'. I didn't understand what that meant, so I asked Gogo, and she tried her best to explain. She said it meant that even if we lived in different households (she in Tottenham and us in Walthamstow), we could still be regarded as a support bubble due to our close contact and connection. The message said people should stay at home, stay indoors, only go out for an hour's exercise, observe social distancing, wash hands frequently, wear face masks outside, and wear hand gloves. My sister and I always sang *The Birthday Song* whilst washing our hands.

Gogo was surprised, and she asked why we sang *The Birthday Song* when washing our hands. We explained that, at school, we were taught to wash our hands for about ten seconds to make sure they were cleaned properly. I explained that, for me, singing *The Birthday Song* was easier than counting.

Gogo told me that when she was growing up as a young girl in Africa, her mother always insisted on her and her siblings keeping their hands clean, especially after using the toilet. So for her, it was not a new practice to wash hands well and regularly. I asked what was new for her in the lockdown, and she said that wearing hand gloves and masks was new. She laughed and said that wearing a mask felt like pretending to be a bank robber.

I asked her about going out for exercise only because I hoped that someone would take us to the local park. Gogo told me that in Africa, children used to play outside a lot and inhale a lot of fresh air. In her South African home and most of the others, the houses were kept clean. Children were not allowed to jump on beds or play with cushions in the living room like we did here. Anyway, she said she understood why children in the UK spent a lot of time indoors. She said the weather was not always suitable for playing outside. The rain stopped children from being up and about. She said she felt sorry for us because where she grew up, the weather was always good, and children ran around without their parents having to worry about their safety. Most parents, even the neighbours, always kept an eye on all youngsters. Of course, she said, things have changed a lot nowadays. She said the village used to look after all children, which sounded quite strange to me, but I said nothing, wondering how people who were not your close family could care for you. That's another thing she said about the differences between European and African cultures.

Anyway, Gogo decided to make homemade masks. She enlisted our help, and we excitedly agreed. We used Gogo's old scarves to sew them.

My older sister thinks she is different from me as she's four years older. When she washes her hands, she does not sing The Happy Birthday Song. She thinks it's for babies despite the fact I've told her so many times that I'm not a baby anymore. Instead, she sings Alicia Keys' song called 'This Girl is on Fire'.

Gogo was surprised at this. She asked her how she knew that song, and worst of all, how she came to know Alicia Keys. The American singer is the same age as our mother (i.e., in her early or middle thirties). According to us, she's old. Anyway, Gogo and I were impressed, and Gogo went on to video tape my sister singing the song. She sang it very well and very loudly. Actually, I thought she was screaming. Her voice invaded my ears. She is also quite the performer.

Even though I was a bit jealous, I went on to applaud her, which is not always the case as she and I always fight for attention, especially from Gogo.

Once we arrived in Tottenham, our daily schedules changed. The worst was that we couldn't attend school, and we missed our school friends a lot. The good thing was that it was summer. Because we couldn't go out a lot, my mummy bought a huge trampoline. Luckily, Gogo has a garden big enough to accommodate the trampoline. During the day, we spent a lot of time jumping on it and screaming at the top of our voices. Sometimes, Gogo got a bit worried.

I suppose that's what old people are like: everything worries them. She told my mummy there were reports alluding to the risks associated with trampolines, and she reckoned an adult needed to supervise the play to identify and prevent problems before they happened. Apparently, there have been reports of children injuring themselves and needing to be taken to hospitals after breaking one thing or another. I must confess I wished I could break a bone or two so that I could be admitted into hospital. The idea of being in hospital and being looked after by doctors and nurses fascinates me. On TV, I saw children in hospital lying in hospital beds. They looked like they were enjoying themselves with all the attention they were getting.

Gogo and my mother took turns sitting outside, watching us scream ourselves sick. Gogo expressed surprise about the screaming. She said that maybe we needed to exercise our vocal cords, but Gogo seemed to be surprised and concerned about a lot of things.

I asked her why that was.

She laughed and said that maybe it was because she had forgotten how young children behave. Her own children were so old that she couldn't remember what they used to do or say when they were young.

I said that maybe it was also because she was so old.

She screwed her face and said, 'Look here, young lady— I'm not that old because I can still hula hoop.' Of course, I must admit that Gogo hula hoops better than I can.

While indoors, my sister tended to spend time on her iPad chatting to her friends, and whilst she allowed me to watch in most cases, she sometimes told me to go away and play on my own somewhere else. Usually, my mother was also busy working on her laptop, so the only person who appeared to be free was Gogo. She has some equipment for exercising, and she does them first thing in the morning. They're very simple exercises, such as basic yoga. She said that older people don't need to do ferocious exercises. A little movement here and there is good enough for them, even I could tell how basic they were.

In the beginning, I used to join her, but I found them a little bit boring, so I took out other equipment such as an exercise mat or weights. I think I got good at lifting weights.

My sister laughed and said I was just mucking about, to which I always responded that it was better than nothing, taking a leaf from Gogo's book (i.e., in the same way that Gogo justified her basic exercises). The most enjoyable exercise I liked engaging in was the hula hoop, even though I wasn't very good at it. Also, it was the activity my sister enjoyed the most, so she usually joined us. She probably liked it because she was better at it than Gogo and me. Though I didn't mind, I needed to practise more, so by the time I left Tottenham, I would be better than my sister, whose smug face I'd like to slap. Granted, she could hula hoop longer than anybody, but Gogo always encouraged me to practise whilst my sister showed off how good she was. Believe me, I love my sister to bits, but she can sometimes be a pain in the butt. Instead, I sometimes went off to muck about on the piano and played keys though I didn't know which notes I played.

One day, Gogo said we needed a structure for our evenings. It was not good enough to sit around, googling on our iPads or watching non-educational stuff on TV, as she referred to our choice of TV programmes. She suggested that we start reading books. Fortunately, my sister and I love reading—or maybe my sister more than me, but that's because she reads better than I do.

I realised that her mission in life was to be better than me. At four years older than me, she sounds old. That must count for something. Though I read well in my own way, I still spell out words before I read them out loud, which sometimes takes a long time and can be boring, but that was how I was taught to read at school.

Gogo called it phonetics or sounds and said that was how she was taught in primary school when she was young. She was impressed at how hard I tried and at the improvements I made. I was also pleased with myself.

Gogo laughed when I told her that practice made perfect. She said, 'That's the spirit.' Gogo has a whole library of books in her bedroom, but most are adult books. She suggested that maybe we should visit the local library to search for books for our age.

I asked her why she had so many books in her bedroom. I've seen other people with shelves full of books in their living rooms.

She said there was a reason she decided to keep them where they were; it was a very safe space. She said it prevented people from asking to loan them and ending up not returning them. More often, she can never remember who she loaned them to. She said that was her experience, and she no longer wanted to take that chance.

I asked her about the countless number of CDs and DVDs she had lined up on shelves in her living room—was she not worried they might be nicked?

She laughed and said, 'In life, you must lose some things.' For some reason, she seemed to place more importance on books than music. She said her books were irreplaceable, but you could always replace CDs, and nobody watches DVDs nowadays anyway, she said. They are all onto Netflix and all that stuff.

We visited the Marcus Garvey Library at Tottenham Leisure Centre and got some books for ourselves. I am afraid there weren't a lot of people there. In the area earmarked for children, there were only about two children. All of the adults in the library wore masks, but not the children.

When we got home, I was the first to read from a book called 'The Day Gogo Went to Vote'. It was a story told by a young girl about the day her gogo went to vote in South Africa's first elections for a Black president, Mr Mandela. Gogo explained that during the elections in SA in 1994, most Black people were voting for the first time in their lives. Most of them voted for a party called the African National Congress (ANC).

In the book, this Gogo was one of the oldest people who went to vote. She was one hundred years old! My sister and I were surprised, but we said nothing. I could not imagine anybody being that old. I tried to count to a hundred on my fingertips, but I just got tired.

Gogo asked if we knew what party she normally voted for in the UK.

My clever clot sister said the Labour Party.

Then, Gogo asked if we knew who the UK prime minister was.

Again, clever clot said Boris Johnson.

I said that I knew that anyway. Of course, I had no idea.

My sister said I didn't, I said I did, and it went on like a Yo-Yo for some time until Gogo said to stop and concentrate on reading.

When it was my sister's turn to read, I decided to act out what she was reading. Whilst she read, I followed her reading with basic yoga movements and ballerina moves.

Gogo said, 'What a better and entertaining way to read,' so, of course, I did my utmost to perform. Anything to outshine sister dearest.

The other book I picked up at the library was called 'How We Love Our Hair'. This book teaches us, especially Black girls, the basics about caring for your hair. Gogo said it could have good tips for all sorts of hair, but it was written precisely for Black girls with curly and knotted hair like mine and my sister's. Gogo said the book was written by somebody called J Ayoola and the designs were by Pelumi I.

I mention this because Gogo always taught us to make a note of the author, illustrator, and publisher when we read books. She said that when we wrote our own books, we would have to know who would publish our books. That was very important, she said, and we needed to choose carefully.

Anyway, that book was about a little Black girl who loved her hair and showed what she could do with it. I recommend that all Black girls read this book because it's a sure way to maintain good hair. The author said that to keep hair soft and manageable, you needed to water it like you do your flowers and plants. That meant drinking water regularly as it ensured the water in your body would travel all the way to the hair on your head. She also recommended a solution made of rosewater, vegetable glycerine, and water, of course. There are all sorts of other ingredients such as coconut oil, aloe vera, and more, mentioned in the book.

My sister and I learned a lot about how to manage our hair from that book. Our poor mum spends a lot of time plaiting our hair to ensure it stays manageable and neat and tidy. Even though I always feel sorry for myself sitting there for hours with her plaiting cornrows or long thing plaits, I feel sorry that she has to spend so much of her time trying to make us look pretty. She says her mum didn't worry herself with this practice as she used to take her to hairdressers or hair salons. She used to pay a lot of money to these people. On the other hand, my mother decided to practise plaiting our hair herself rather than paying a lot of money on hair salon fees. Fortunately, she improved the skill, and she is so much better at it, and she is doing a fabulous job, for that matter.

The most important part of that book was how, as young girls, we could practically manage our curly hair ourselves. We started experimenting on ourselves while playing around with it. We parted the hair in sections and rubbed and creamed it with solutions, leaving it feeling super- fluffy. We parted it in large sections and twisted and braided it as we went along. Sometimes, we left it in huge, broad sections, which my cousins in South Africa refer to as 'Ben and Betty'. Why it's that name is a mystery to me. The advice in that book was very exciting and entertaining for us, and it really kept us busy and brought us closer to our natural hair.

My mum bought Gogo an Alexa for her birthday. Gogo said it was the best present she ever had. She plays mainly jazz and/or smooth FM radio. Whatever she does in the room, the music serenades her in the background. Because she lives alone, she says it is like having a friend in the house with her, and it keeps her company.

One day, a song came up from an American film called Harriet. It turned out that we knew the song, and my sister and I started singing along. Gogo was so excited listening to us that she went on to video tape us. We belted out the song as if it belonged to us, with my sister, of course, singing—or should I say screaming the loudest—the song as if it were her last day on earth. Gogo then forwarded the video to our family in SA.

I asked if it went viral, and Gogo said yes, but I knew she was just joking. We were just so pleased that we had sung along as Gogo was always listening to it. I'm glad, particularly because Gogo can keep herself occupied listening to the music as she reads the books lining the shelves in her bedroom library.

I told her that it felt like treasure was buried in her bedroom.

She laughed and said it was real treasure buried in her bedroom. She told me that her things would be passed on to us as a legacy. Of course, I'd rather have money instead, but conventional wisdom tells us not to look a gift horse in the mouth.

On some occasions, my cousin and his younger brother came to visit. His name is Aydryan. His middle name is Rethabile, an African name. I asked Gogo what it meant, and she said it was like her name, Nthabiseng. Both names had more or less the same meaning. She said African names always had a meaning. My cousin's name means 'we are all happy or in a state of being comfortable'. Gogo's name means 'make me happy or come over and enjoy and be happy with me'.

Gogo decided we needed a bit of teaching when it came to the African language. When she asked us what second languages we were taught at school, we said we weren't, but when she said which second languages we wished to learn, she was pleasantly surprised that my sister and I simultaneously said, 'An African language.'

She said that, in that case, it made her job much easier. She said it was a good thing to know different languages and that people from other cultures and countries loved it when you tried to speak their language. She said that if you want to be welcome in a different country, the secret was to try to speak the local language.

Before my sister visited SA for the first time a few years ago, Gogo taught her two ditties. One was a lullaby in IsiZulu, called 'Thula-, thula sanalwam', which means hush-hush baby. The other one was in SeSotho called 'Bana ba sekolo ', translated as the ding dong bell song, calling children to attend school. She also knew other African phrases such as hello, good morning, how are you, and so on, which made my sister into a little celebrity when she started showing off her accomplishments in South Africa.

I followed Gogo everywhere in her house, and I asked a lot of questions about everything. Sometimes, she said she didn't know the answers to some of my questions.

I asked how come she's lived such a long time and still didn't know some things. I told her that when I'm her age, I'll know everything under the sun.

She laughed, took my arm, sat me next to her, and said, 'Little one, nobody knows everything. This is a lesson you need to learn. The more you learn, the more you discover you know ziltz.'

I laughed at that and said, 'What is ziltz?' even though I could work out what it meant. I told Gogo that I was the cleverest girl amongst the top four boys in my class.

She said it is good to have confidence, but it is better to be humble.

Whenever Gogo went to the bathroom, I would knock on the door, and she always said there was someone in there. She asked why it was that every time she wanted to use the facilities, there was always a little person who wanted to use them as well, precisely at the time when she was using it.

My sister did it, too. She said it was like when she was on the phone and suddenly, some little person wanted attention. Apparently, my mother and her brothers used to do that, too.

Anyway, I sat on a small step outside the toilet and asked what she was doing.

As if I didn't know, she said.

I asked if she was doing number one or number two, which means either a wee or a poo.

She said none of the two, to which I said, 'It must be number three, then.'

Surprisingly, she said, 'What's number three?'

I said, 'Diarrhoea.' I'm surprised she didn't know.

She laughed and said, 'Where did you hear that?'

I said to her, 'See? I know more things than you do.'

I asked how long she was going to be in there.

She said, 'Ten minutes,' so I sat out there, counting to ten.

After a count of ten, I told her that time was up.

She said, 'Ten minutes is not the same as counting to ten." This baffled me. Anyway, I waited patiently outside the door.

Eventually, when she came out, I said, 'Wow! You took your time in there.'

She said to me, 'You know what? I feel like I'm under surveillance of some kind.' I asked what that meant, and she said, 'You're like a shadow. I look behind me, and there you are.' We both laughed because that sounded funny.

My sister came out of her room and asked what was going on. As always, her curiosity got the better of her, and she loved to be a part of the fun. For a moment, she left the company of her iPad, only because my mum was monitoring how long she spent on it.

I told her that it was a secret, and Gogo agreed, so we kept her wondering. It served her right to be so nosy because when she's on her iPad, she is oblivious to anything and anybody around her.

Gogo was sitting in the living room, minding her own business, one of those rare moments when she could enjoy her privacy. I interrupted her thoughts to tell her that I knew words that rhymed.

She said, 'Oh, that's interesting,' and she asked, 'what they are?'

Enthusiastically I went, "Mat, cat, hat, bat, pat, and rat.'

Gogo seemed impressed that I knew so many of them, so she told me that when she was my age or maybe younger, she could make a sentence with those words. I challenged her to do it, so she said, 'De cat sat on de mat.'

I was tickled pink because she sounded so funny. I asked why she sounded so funny, and she said that it was supposed to be funny because, as a primary school kid in South Africa, she didn't know how to speak English properly. She had to learn to speak it, and it wasn't easy because English, unlike other languages, is difficult to understand with its word constructions. In most languages, what you see written is what you pronounce, but no, not English. She remembered how the children in her class used to want to show off by speaking English. As she was in a Roman Catholic school, most of her teachers were white nuns who mainly spoke English. So, the little ones used to like to impress them by saying incomprehensible sentences like, 'Is shebberi as shebberi is laat.' What that meant to her and the others was anybody's guess. We both laughed, and I said it must have been exciting.

My sister and I liked to raid Gogo's bedroom. We went through her drawers, took out all the jewellery, and tried it on. My sister likes arts and crafts——she always leaves a mess behind. She doesn't mind using anything at her disposal to create stuff. As a result, she always got us into trouble with Gogo. She's one of those children described as creative, but most often, you can call it being messy. On the other hand (i.e., if you don't mind the mess), she's really creative. She likes to dirty her hands. Sometimes, she comes up with really impressive stuff like when we created thank you postcards for the NHS staff.

Every Thursday evening, we used to stand on the front porch in Gogo's front yard with all of the neighbours on the street, and we used to clap hands for NHS nurses and doctors. My sister and I would go out with Gogo's vuvuzelas, (blow pipes that look like Scottish bagpipes) and blow our lungs out whilst the neighbours banged on tins and bins. There was such a racket; we really enjoyed those moments.

One of the ways Gogo created structure for us was by encouraging us to learn to play the piano. There was one in the house, and somebody needed to use it. Ironically Gogo's own children started learning but gave up when they became serious with their studies, so she wanted to make sure that at least one of her grandchildren took it up.

My sister was being tutored in piano, but because of the pandemic, she was learning by Zoom. She enjoyed the lessons, but in our home at Walthamstow, she played on a keyboard, which was not the same as practising on a real piano.

I preferred practising the hula hoop. Gogo bought us these hula hoops, and they stayed in Tottenham. She taught my sister, and so I was also in the process of learning. There are four of these hula hoops in Gogo's house, two large and two small. My cousin practised on them, as well, when he came to visit. I was surprised that he was better than me, but I'm getting there slowly and gradually.

Gogo encouraged me. She also hula hoops, but the pro in the house was my sister; she could go on for more than an hour.

At some point during the pandemic, there was an announcement from the government that the levels of COVID were going down, and it looked like restrictions might be lifted. At that point, my mum was having difficulty home tutoring us and doing her job from home at the same time. It turned out that we would be allowed to return to school. The reason for this was that my dad was classified as an essential worker, so his children were allowed to return to school.

My daddy works as an electrical engineer, digging electrical poles around London. I'm sure there's more to this job than I can explain. Most of the time, he comes back home with dirty overalls and boots that sometimes smell.

Gogo did not like the smell, and she advised my dad that whenever he visited, he should leave his overalls and boots outside the house before entering. She explained that men had it easy in this country because there were showers and plenty of water everywhere. She said that, in her time in South Africa, African men used to (and still do) dig in mines for gold and diamonds as part of their jobs. They came out of those long, deep holes with soot all over them, but when they got home, they had to leave what they were wearing outside the door because African women took pride in their homes when it concerned standards of hygiene and cleanliness. The men would have to clean themselves thoroughly in buckets of water. At that point during the apartheid era, there were no showers or baths for Black people in the country. Unfortunately, as well, she didn't live near a river or sea where people could go, just dive in, and soak themselves with ease.

My mum decided that we should go back to school, which meant going back to our home in Walthamstow, as well. So, we had to prepare ourselves. I must say that my sister and I were quite excited because we missed our teachers and friends. At the same time, we were unhappy to leave Gogo alone. I suspected she would miss us as well, but I was also relieved that she could take things easy again, like waking up any time she wished and daydreaming as much as she wanted without having little monkeys asking her all sorts of questions. It was a huge mix of feelings for all of us to return to our normal routines. We were always—or should I say, I was always—waking her up earlier than she was used to.

Waking up at 6 a.m. for someone who was not going to work was bound to be difficult. Gogo said she felt like taking a long holiday after we visited her. She complained about being exhausted. So, though she was going to miss us, she was also looking forward to regaining her space and enjoying her privacy. She said the company of little people like us should be timed. As she was of a certain age and had mobility problems, it was a good idea not to overdo things such as us being with her longer than was necessary. She said that she had brought up her children in a foreign country without support from an extended family, and her children should do likewise. Of course, she didn't mind helping out every now and again. She said that when she grew up in

South Africa, children were considered everybody's children, and her neighbours took on the responsibility of raising other people's children. In a sense, a child being raised by the village was the norm, but we live in different times and circumstances. Nowadays, children are warned about strangers, and there is no longer freedom of movement, especially for children. Wherever you go in this country, be it at a park, swimming pool, or any public place, there are signs giving advice that children should be accompanied by an adult.

The night before we left, Gogo decided that we needed to create memory boxes. As usual, I did not know what she meant, but it made sense after she explained. All good or not-so-good memories of our stay in her house needed to be kept safe in 'memory boxes'. She said that when we grow older, it will be important to remember our stories and histories so we can share them with others. She said that was part of our identity.

We liked the idea, and so we got going. It was right up my sister's street as she liked to create things, and I always love a challenge!!!!

We started off creating a collage of all the cards Gogo had been keeping safe for as long as she could remember. There were all sorts of cards: Xmas, birthday, Mother's Day, and hundreds of sympathy cards she'd received after Granddad's death. She said she had found it difficult to throw them away.

I asked her if it was an old people's thing not to get rid of stuff. I only asked because she also refused to let me to pop her birthday balloons days after her birthday.

Gogo replied that sometimes, some things carry a lot of sentiment, so they become difficult to get rid of. She said that I would understand that when I grew older, but it is still a mystery to me.

For the next step, we moved to choosing items for our memory boxes, three in all: one for me, another for my sister, and the last for Gogo. We used shoe boxes. I put everything I could think of in there, but because the boxes weren't that big, Gogo advised that the idea was to store memorable and sentimental stuff. I had difficulty choosing, but I eventually had to.

My sister cracked on, but as usual, she was being cagey about what she was keeping safe in her box. She wouldn't let on what she was putting in her box, saying it was a mystery or more of a secret, I suppose.

Gogo chose a few important cards she thought meant something to her. All boxes were half-filled hoping that the next time we visited, we would bring along some new stuff of sentimental value, as Gogo explained.

The day arrived when we were ready to move back to our home and go back to school. The car was packed full of our stuff, and Gogo commented that she'd never seen a small family like us with so much stuff. She referred to my mother as a 'bag lady', always carrying things.

We left with a mixture of emotions, both excitement, and sorrow. One thing I wanted to say about my Gogo but could not say at the time was that she is a very kind person. She bought us things that small people liked. For instance, I like chocolates, and my sister likes meat; Gogo never fails to cook chicken wings, pork chops, salmon, lamb chops, and more. She always takes us on a visit to the South African shop in Barking, where we buy biltong (dried cured beef), my sister's favourite, but it is not such a delicacy for me.

I always choose chewing gum. It's called chappies in South Africa. Gogo made us aware that the wrapping on the chewing gum has general knowledge. For instance, I did not know that South Africa was the biggest producer and exporter of diamonds and gold until I read it on the wrapper.

Gogo said this knowledge was sometimes not taught in UK schools. She said the biggest diamond in the world was from South Africa, and it was called the Cullinan, named after the white English man who was the manager of a diamond mine in Pretoria, Johannesburg. The Black man who found the diamond is not mentioned in the records. Nobody knew what his name was, where he was, or what happened to him.

Gogo is not only generous, but she is strict, as well. She likes to keep boundaries. She said she liked teaching us what we were not taught in school or by our parents. She called it an 'informal education'.

She made us tidy up after messing up. We sat still at the dining table and couldn't watch our iPad at the same time. We took our plates to the kitchen after eating. I always got into trouble with Gogo because I didn't always remember. She told me that I was a messy eater. My side of the table and my chair were always left with bits and pieces of food after I'd finished eating. At nine years old, she said my sister should have already started learning how to wash the dishes. However, at Gogo's, she ended up stacking the dishes in the dishwasher. She was surprised that my sister didn't like doing that anymore but when she was my age —five years old— I understand that she always asked to do little jobs, but I suppose, as she grew up, she found new areas of interest.

At last, we left Tottenham, feeling better than when we had arrived. We learn a lot from our visit. We left with good memories, and I hope we can always remember that learning is a process that reveals new ideas and never ends, thanks to my Gogo's wisdom.

About the Author

Nthabi is a retired social worker and grandmother to Palesa and Nehanda. She wrote this book during lockdown whilst living with her daughter and two grandchildren. Before that, she was living all alone without much company and feeling sorry for herself.

Nthabi enjoys reading and has a huge collection of books in her house. Nthabi enjoys teaching the girls her native South African language and songs, as well as traditional values.

Despite her ankle problems, Nthabi also likes to keep fit by walking in the park with her 85-year-old neighbour, Lily, swimming twice a week and doing yoga. However, during lockdown, she learnt how to hula hoop with the girls!

About the Author

Nehanda is Palesa's little sister and together are very close even though they tend to argue just like most siblings do. Generally, Nehanda is inquisitive and always wants to learn new things. Unlike her older sister, she is forever asking questions and pressing for answers.

She has a lot of friends at school and is generally a team player. At home, she likes to help with cooking and dishing out food. She is involved in a lot of after-school activities such as cookery, swimming, and karate and recently she's joined tennis training.

About the Illustrator

Palesa is creative and artistic. She has spent much of her young life interested in drawing anything under the sun. Give her a pen, paper and crayons, and she will spend her time scribbling away. She draws people and landscapes. Her outstanding talent is how vividly she can draw people's eyes. In addition to drawing, she's passionate about painting and creating things out of scraps of materials.

At the start of writing this book with her grandmother and sister, Palesa was nine years old. Now she is eleven. Palesa is also a sports enthusiast who loves participating in the school morning forest run and has weekly netball, karate and swimming practice. She has a lot of friends, loves music, dancing and enjoys playing the piano.

Conscious Dreams
PUBLISHING

Transforming diverse writers into
successful published authors

  www.consciousdreamspublishing.com

  authors@consciousdreamspublishing.com

Let's connect

www.ingramcontent.com/pod-product-compliance
Lightning Source LLC
Chambersburg PA
CBHW070339120526
44590CB00017B/2949